MW00710996

As Christ Is
My Example

A Daily Walk in Faith with Christ

Denise,
    May God continue
        To bless you!
        Love, your friend,
        Jan Keegan 9/15/13

Jan Keegan

CROSSBOOKS
PUBLISHING

CrossBooks™
A Division of LifeWay
1663 Liberty Drive
Bloomington, IN 47403
www.crossbooks.com
Phone: 1-866-879-0502

Art and Design Illustration
By
Heather H. Hatheway

First published by CrossBooks 6/21/2013

ISBN: 978-1-4627-2900-5 (sc)
ISBN: 978-1-4627-2901-2 (e)

Printed in the United States of America.

This book is printed on acid-free paper.

TABLE OF CONTENTS

PREFACE

The purpose of this book is to help us understand the teachings of Christ better and to understand the type of life He lived while here on earth. His life and teachings are written in the four Gospel Books of the Bible, Matthew, Mark, Luke, and John. In these books, Christ provided examples either in His teachings or in His daily activities of how we should live our lives as His followers. Being able to learn and understand these examples should help provide direction and guidance to us as we strive to live and grow in our Christian faith.

BIBLICAL SCRIPTURE

Christ, our Lord, said, "For I have set you an example, that you also should do as I have done to you." John 13:15 NRS.

Christ, our Lord, said, "Very truly, I tell you, the one who believes in me will also do the works that I do...." John 14:12a NRS.

Christ, our Lord, said, "But strive first for Kingdom of God...." Matthew 6:33a NRS.8

Peter, an apostle of Christ said, "For to this you have been called, because Christ also suffered for you, leaving you an example, so that you should follow in his steps." 1 Peter 2:21 NRS.

Day 1   PRAYER

As Christ is my example,

I will rise early and go to a quiet place. There I will spend time with the Father, praying and meditating, listening for His word and direction. Mark 1:35 NRS says, "In the morning, while it is still very dark, He got up and went out to a deserted place, and there He prayed." Christ, our Lord, began His day by rising early, going to a quiet place and praying to the Father. As Christ in my example, I too will arise early and begin my day by praying to the Father.

Day 2   REST

As Christ is my example,

I will go away to a deserted place and rest. I will be by myself, giving mind and body rest from the stresses and challenges that I am facing. Christ, our Lord, said to His apostles, " 'Come away to a deserted place all by yourselves and rest for a while.' For many were coming and going and they had no leisure even to eat." Mark 6:31b NRS. Christ knew what it meant to be tired and stressed. He knew that rest was important in order to be able to function and carry out His service here on earth. As Christ is my example, I will get away from the stresses of life and rest my body and mind.

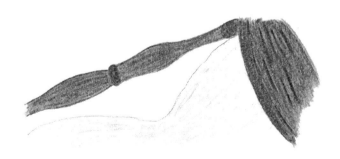

Day 3   SERVICE

As Christ is my example,

I will serve my fellow mankind all the days of my life as I am physically, mentally and spiritually able. Christ, our Lord, said, "The Son of Man came not to be served but to serve…." Matthew 20:28a NRS. Christ served others throughout His life on earth. He washed the disciples feet. He fed the thousands bread and fish. He comforted the weary and the heavy-burdened. As Christ is my example, I will serve others in whatever capacity I am capable, whether it is providing bread for my fellow man, providing comfort to those in distress or showing love to my neighbor. As Christ is my example, I will serve my fellow mankind.

Day 4   HUMBLENESS

As Christ is my example,

I will humble myself in my relationships with others. Christ, our Lord, said, "Take my yoke upon you, and learn from me; for I am gentle and humble in heart…." Matthew 11:29 a. NRS. Throughout His life, Christ provided an example of His humble spirit when choosing to dine with the tax collectors and sinners, healing the sick and disabled, feeding the hungry and comforting the poor. I will strive to do away with my self-righteous, prideful attitude, trying not to be judgmental or critical, humbling myself, as Christ is my example.

Day 5   FORGIVENESS

As Christ is my
example,

I will strive to forgive
others when they hurt
me causing me pain and suffering. Christ, our Lord, said
as He hung from the cross, "Father, forgive them, for
they do not know what they are doing…." Luke 23:34
NRS. Christ taught forgiveness during His ministry
because He knew that ill feelings towards another
would interfere with the unity that is needed among
Christians to do Christ's work here on earth. In one
of His teachings, Christ was asked about forgiveness
of a brother and He said "….Not seven times, but, I
tell you seventy-seven times". Matthew 18:22 NRS;
emphasizing the need for a forgiving heart. Christ shed
his blood for the forgiveness of our sins. Learning to
forgive is a hard process to develop. Forgiveness of
another often takes Christ's power working though us
to help forgive another. We may have to ask for Christ's
help when forgiving one who has hurt us. As Christ is
my example, I will strive to forgive others.

Day 6   TEMPTATION

As Christ is my example,

I will use the Word of God to get past the many temptations that I face on a daily basis. When my thoughts dwell on an idea I know is wrong, I will quote a Bible verse to break that thought process from continuing. Matthew 4:3-4 NRS says, "The tempter came and said to him, "If you are the Son of God, command these stones to become loaves of bread." But Christ answered, "It is written, 'One does not live by bread alone but by every Word that comes from the mouth of God.' " Christ was quoting scripture to the tempter written several hundred years before Christ was born, from Deuteronomy 8:3b NRS. I will train myself with Bible verses when I am tempted so that I can say a verse to direct my thoughts away from temptation, as Christ is my example.

Day 7   COMPASSION

As Christ is my example,

I will have compassion for those that are physically, mentally or spiritually in pain and distress. When Christ, our Lord, saw the crowds, "He had compassion for them, because they were harassed and helpless, like sheep without a shepherd." Matthew 9:36b NRS. Throughout His ministry, Christ was ministering to crowds of people through His teaching and healing, showing compassion to those who were suffering. As Christ is my example, I will have compassion for those that are in pain and distress.

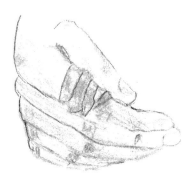

Day 8   LOVE

As Christ is my example,

I will love my fellow mankind. Christ, our Lord, said, "This is my commandment, that you love one another as I have loved you." John 15:12 NRS. Christ showed His love to mankind throughout His life, as well as in His death and resurrection. The depth of His love has survived through the hundred of years and can be felt today when one studies His life and ministry while here on earth as well as the love shown by Christian followers of Christ's example. As Christ is my example, I will love my fellow mankind.

Day 9 MERCY

As Christ is my example,

I will show mercy to my fellow man. Christ, our Lord, said "Go home to your friends and tell them how much the Lord has done for you, and what mercy he has shown you." Mark 5:19b NRS. Christ showed mercy to His fellow man when He walked on earth, teaching and healing the many. Time after time, in His interaction with individuals, He showed mercy, love and compassion, forgiving those who were hurtful and spiteful to Him. He instructed us to do the same. As Christ is my example, I will show mercy to my fellow man.

Day 10   WORSHIP

As Christ is my example,

I will attend church on the Sabbath. Luke 4:16b says that Christ, our Lord "went to the synagogue on the Sabbath as was his custom." Christ went to the synagogue to worship God. He knew that through worship, He would draw nearer to God. Through worship, we learn and grow as Christians. Praying, singing, praising or listening to a sermon brings us closer to God and each other. Worship helps unify our common beliefs and goals so that we may do Christ's work here on earth. As Christ is my example, I will attend church on the Sabbath to worship God.

Day 11   PERSECUTION

As Christ is my example,

I will suffer persecution for my belief and faith in Christ. Christ, our Lord said, "Blessed are those who are persecuted for righteousness sake, for theirs is the kingdom of heaven." Matthew 5:10 NRS. Christ was persecuted throughout His life of ministry for speaking the truth, going against the popular mode of thinking, doing the will of his Father. As Christ is my example, I will suffer persecution for my belief and faith in Christ.

Day 12   GENTLENESS

As Christ is my example,

I will be gentle in my dealings with others. Christ describes himself as a person who is "gentle and humble in heart." Matthew 11:29b NRS. We know by studying His life and by His own description, that Christ was a gentle man. No harsh or rude reaction. No critical or impatient reply or answer. As Christ is my example, I will be gentle in my dealing with others.

Day 13   TAKE UP MY CROSS

As Christ is my example,

I will strive to take up my cross daily. Christ, our Lord, said, "If any want to be My followers, let them deny themselves and take up their cross daily and follow Me." Luke 9:23 NRS. Christ took up His cross on calvary for our sakes, to save us from our sins and to give us a new life in Him. He knew that if we wanted to be His followers, we would have to deny ourselves of our selfish wants and desires; and follow his teachings. As Christ is my example, I will strive to take up my cross daily, denying myself and my selfish desires so that I may become His follower and follow Him all the days of my life.

Day 14   THE WORD OF GOD

As Christ is my example,

I will read the Word of God increasing my knowledge of God, through His written word, the Holy Bible. Christ, our Lord, "stood up to read, and the scroll of the prophet Isaiah was given to Him. He unrolled the scroll and found the place where it was written…." Luke 4:16b-17 NRS. Throughout His ministry, Christ quoted from the Old Testament of the Bible to help Him in His teachings. In order to quote the scripture, Christ had to be knowledgeable in the Word of God. In Luke 24: 44b-45 NRS, Christ said…." that everything written about me in the law of Moses, the prophets and psalms must be fulfilled. Then He opened their minds to understand the scriptures…." As Christ is my example, I will read the Word of God, the Holy Bible, and increase my knowledge of God by studying His writings

Day 15 LOVE OF NATURE

As Christ is my example,

I will love and respect nature in my daily living. Christ, our Lord, said, "Consider the lilies of the field, how they grow: they neither toil or spin, yet I tell you, even Solomon in all his glory was not clothed like these." Matthew 6:28b-29 NRS. Throughout His teachings, Christ referred to nature, talking about the birds of the air, using the harvest of the wheat, describing the sowing of the seed, using soil and rocks in his parables. He discussed the weather, in one instance, and calmed the storm in another instance. Christ spent time near the Sea of Galilee and in the fields and hills that surrounded it. He was aware of nature, using nature in His teachings. As Christ is my example, I will love and respect nature in my daily living.

Day 16   THE WILL OF GOD

As Christ is my example,

I will strive to do the will of God in my daily life. Christ, our Lord, said "I will seek to do not my own will but the will of Him who sent me." John 5:30b NRS. As Christ followed the will of God throughout His life, so I will try to learn what God's will is for my life and seek to do His will in all that I do. We often ask, "How do I know what God's will is for me?" We can learn God's will for us by learning God's ways as described in the Bible, by learning God's commandments and by praying to God, listening for His small voice to give us direction in our lives. As Christ is my example, I will strive to do the will of God in my life.

Day 17   GLORIFYING GOD

As Christ is my example,

I will strive to glorify God with my life. I will make my decisions based on glorifying God. Christ, our Lord, said in His prayer to God, "I glorify you on earth by finishing the work that you gave me to do." John 17:4 NRS. Throughout His life, in all the different aspects of His works, whether it was teaching, preaching or healing; Christ glorified God in all that He did. To glorify God is God's greatest desire from us. To exalt His name, to hold Him as the highest, to place Him first; this is glorifying God. As Christ is my example, I will strive to glorify God in all that I do.

Day 18   HUMAN NATURE

As Christ is my example,

I will be aware of human nature, realizing that I, too, am human with all of the weaknesses that humans have. Christ, our Lord, said "....when people hate you, and when they exclude you, revile you and defame you"…. Luke 6: 22 NRS. In another instance, Christ our Lord, said "For it is from within, from the human heart, that evil intentions come…." Mark 7:21a NRS. Christ knew the mind and heart of the person, and the natural thoughts and actions of the person in all kinds of situations. In John 2: 24-25 NRS, the scripture says, "But Jesus on His part would not entrust Himself to them, because He knew all people and needed no one to testify about anyone; for He himself knew what was in everyone." This was what His ministry was about, to help us overcome our human weaknesses and live a Christ-like life here on earth, following His example. As Christ is my example, I will strive to know myself and recognize my weaknesses so that I may use His example and teachings in overcoming my weaknesses and living a life that is pleasing to Him.

Day 19 TURNING THE OTHER CHEEK

As Christ is my example,

I will strive to turn the other cheek when I am hurt by another. Christ, our Lord, said, "Do not resist an evildoer. But if anyone strikes you on the right cheek, turn the other also." Matthew 5:39 NRS. Christ demonstrated this action during His trial prior to His crucifixion when He had opportunities to answer and dispute His accusers. He turned the other cheek answering aggression with submission causing the chief judge to say, "….I have not found this man guilty…Luke 23:14b NRS." Christ knew that showing resistance to an evildoer would increase the anger of the one who was striking the cheek. As Christ is my example, I will strive to turn the other cheek when I am hurt or confronted by another.

Day 20   WISDOM

As Christ is my example,

I will try to develop and practice wisdom in my daily walk with God. Christ, our Lord, said, "See, I am sending you out like sheep into the midst of the wolves; so be wise as serpents and innocent as doves." Matthew 10:16 NRS. Christ knew that wisdom gives one the ability to make good judgments in making the kind of decisions that are necessary to live the Christian life. The wisdom of Christ's teachings has been illustrated through the lives of His followers down through the years. As Christ is my example, I will try to develop and practice wisdom in my daily walk with God.

Day 21   WORK

As Christ is my example,

I will strive to work for Christ whenever the opportunity arises. Christ, our Lord, said, "We must work the works of Him who sent me while it is day; night is coming and no one can work." John 9:4 NRS. Christ knew there would be numerous obstacles and circumstances that would occur in our lives that would interfere with our Christian work; and that we would have to take the opportunity to do His work when the opportunity arises, in order to fulfill His purposes. As Christ is my example, I will strive to work for Christ whenever the opportunity arises.

Page 22   COMMANDMENTS

As Christ is my example,

I will learn God's commandments to help me in my everyday living. Christ, our Lord, said, "….for I have not spoken on my own, but the Father who sent me has Himself given me a commandment about what to say and what to speak. And I know that His commandment is eternal life…." John 12:49-50a NRS. By studying what Christ taught, one will learn the ways and commandments of Christ that will give direction and help in facing the challenges of every day day living. As Christ is my example, I will learn God's commandments to help me in my every day living.

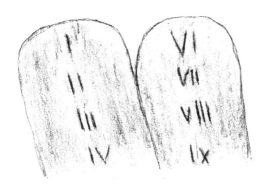

Day 23   FRIENDSHIP

As Christ is my example,

I will consider Christ as my friend. Christ, our Lord, said, "You are my friends if you do what I command you. I do not call you servants any longer, because the servant does not know what the master is doing; but I have called you friends, because I have made known to you everything that I have heard from my Father." John 15:14-15 NRS. To have Christ as my friend is my greatest joy. As Christ is my example, I will accept Christ as my friend and follow what He commands me to do.

Day 24 SIN

As Christ is my example,

I will try my best not to sin. Sin has been defined as any action or thought that goes against God, by not accepting and doing His will for us, being ungrateful for all He has done for us, by not obeying His commandments and by placing ourselves and our desires before His desires for us. We sin against God in our actions toward others. Christ, our Lord, said, …. 'Truly I tell you, just as you did it to one of the least of these who are members of my family, you did it to me…' Matthew 25:40b NRS. We know through our study of Christ's life, that Christ did not sin. In Matthew 5:48 NRS, Christ says,…. "Be perfect, therefore, as your heavenly Father is perfect." As Christ is my example, I will try my best not to sin against God and others.

Day 25   HEALING MINISTRY

As Christ is my example,

I will strive to serve God through helping others who are mentally, physically or spiritually ill. Christ, our Lord, was teaching when "….the power of the Lord was with Him to heal." Luke 5:17 NRS. We know by studying His life, that Christ healed hundreds of people, including those with mental illness [demons], skin problems [leprosy], neurological problems [paralysis], the list could go on and on. Matthew 4:23 NRS, says that Christ went throughout Galilee "….curing every disease and every sickness among the people." As Christ is my example, I will strive to assist those who are ill in whatever way I am able.

Day 26   PROCLAIM THE GOOD NEWS

As Christ is my example,

I will help proclaim the news of Christ in any way I can. Christ, our Lord, said, "I must proclaim the good news of the Kingdom of God to the other cities also; for I was sent for this purpose." Luke 4:43b NRS. Christ's ministry consisted in teaching and preaching using direct instruction, giving commandments and using parables to bring the good news of His redemptive love and saving power to those He was preaching and teaching to. As Christ is my example, I will help to proclaim the good news of Christ's teaching in any way that I can.

Day 27 FAITH

As Christ is my example,

I will have faith in God as I go about my daily activities. Christ, our Lord, said, "For truly I tell you, if you have faith the size of a mustard seed, you will say to the mountain, "move from here to there" and it will move: and nothing will be impossible for you." Matthew 17:20b NRS. Christ, in His healing ministry reinforced the need to have faith in God when He said, "....your faith has saved you." Luke 18:42b NRS. Faith is basic to our Christian life for with faith, one has that inner sense of belief that with God's help, nothing will be impossible. Faith in God is what sustains us through our trials and tribulations. As Christ is my example, I will have faith in God as I go about my daily activities.

Day 28   KNOWLEDGE

As Christ is my example,

I will strive to know God as much as possible. Christ, our Lord, said, "I am the way, and the truth and the life. No one comes to the Father except through me. If you know me, you will know my Father also. From now on you do know him and have seen him." John 14:6b-7 NRS. Through studying Christ's life here on earth, we learn about God and what God expects us to do with our lives, and how to act and behave toward others. Christ taught us that all we need to know to live as Christians, serving and glorifying Him through our daily living. I will strive to know and get closer to God through studying the life of His son, Christ, who is my example.

Day 29 PLEASING GOD

As Christ is my example,

I will strive to please God in all that I do. Christ, our Lord, said, "….for I always do what is pleasing to Him." John 8:29c NRS. Christ taught us through His examples of love, mercy, faithfulness, forgiveness, compassion and sacrifice how to be pleasing to God. Through the study of Christ's life, we can continually learn what is pleasing to Him and live our lives by following His example. As Christ is my example, I will strive to live a life that is pleasing to God.

Day 30 PLACING GOD FIRST

As Christ is my example,

I will place God first in my life. Christ, our Lord, said, "....You should love the Lord your God with all your heart, and with all your soul, and with all your mind. This is the greatest and first commandment." Matthew 22:37a-38 NRS. Christ knew that we go about our lives trying to survive our circumstances and problems, meeting goals and fulfilling needs as we progress through life. He knew how easy it is to place our wants and needs first, without thinking of God or worshiping or honoring Him and His will for our lives. He instructed us to follow this first commandment, by loving God and placing Him first in our lives. As Christ is my example, I will place God first in my life.

Day 31   BE POSITIVE

As Christ is my example,

I will be positive in my attitudes and actions towards others. Christ gave positive, uplifting direction to His followers throughout his teachings. In Matthew 28:19 NSR, Jesus said "Go therefore and make disciples of all Nations…." and in verse 20, "and teaching them to obey everything I have commanded you." In other scriptures in the Gospels, Christ said, "serve," "love," "believe;" all positive actions that are progressive in nature. As Christ is my example, I will be positive in my attitudes and actions towards others.

CPSIA information can be obtained at www.ICGtesting.com
Printed in the USA
LVOW10s0018130713

342623LV00001B/1/P